Trinity College
Dublin

A Beautiful Place

With an Introduction by Thomas N. Mitchell, Provost of Trinity College,
and a Foreword by Brendan Kennelly

Profits from the sale of this book are donated to
Trinity College Dublin Library and Scholarship Funds

Cover image, and I.   Henry Moore's *Reclining Connected Forms* (1969) in the January light.
The view southwestwards across Library Square, between the western end of the Old Library and the
Campanile, towards the 1937 Reading Room.

Trinity College
Dublin

A Beautiful Place

Welcome to
"a friendly and beautiful place"

TRINITY COLLEGE DUBLIN

Trinity College is Ireland's oldest and most famous university, founded by Royal Charter of Queen Elizabeth I in 1592. Originally located well outside the city walls, it now stands at the heart of the city, its beautiful buildings and gracious squares forming a forty-two acre oasis of quiet and learning.

It is famous for the splendour of its eighteenth century Georgian architecture, for its numerous treasures, most notably the magnificent early Christian manuscript, the Book of Kells, which it houses in its great Library, but also for the distinction of its graduates and scholars down the centuries, who number great literary figures such as Swift and Wilde and Beckett, great philosophers such as Berkeley, who gave his name to California's most eminent university, and scientists such as Hamilton, and Walton, the Nobel Laureate whose work made possible the splitting of the atom.

Trinity has produced great leaders too, among them Edmund Burke, Henry Grattan, Wolfe Tone, Ireland's first President, Douglas Hyde, and its first woman President, Mary Robinson.

Trinity is proud of its past but is not constrained by it. Today it is famous for the quality of its teaching and research, a modern university of the first rank with a student body in excess of 14,000, drawn from all parts of Ireland and from more than sixty countries overseas. It offers degree courses across the range of disciplines, in the Humanities, Social Sciences, Sciences, Engineering and Health Sciences, and its professional degrees cover Law, Pharmacy, Dentistry, Medicine and a range of other areas of the Health Sciences.

It is a residential College, its students living in the squares in the heart of the campus, creating a vibrant, collegiate ambience which fosters social fellowship and promotes learning outside as well as inside the classroom.

It is a friendly and beautiful place, and this book seeks to capture its spirit and its charm and to provide a pleasing memento of its historical and cultural riches.

Thomas N. Mitchell
Provost, Trinity College, Dublin

February 2000

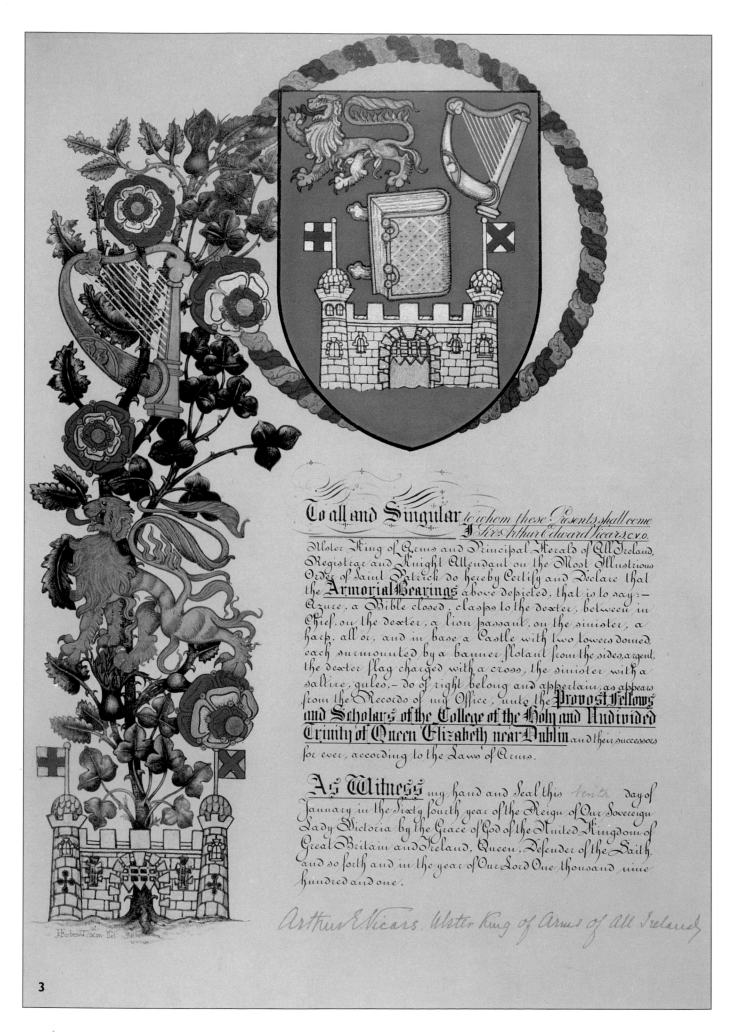

To all and Singular _to whom these Presents shall come_ I _Sir Arthur Edward Vicars_, C.V.O. Ulster King of Arms and Principal Herald of All Ireland, Registrar and Knight Attendant on the Most Illustrious Order of Saint Patrick do hereby Certify and Declare that the **Armorial Bearings** above depicted, that is to say:— Azure, a Bible closed, clasps to the dexter, between in Chief, on the dexter, a lion passant, on the sinister, a harp, all or, and in base a Castle with two towers domed, each surmounted by a banner flotant from the sides, argent, the dexter flag charged with a cross, the sinister with a saltire, gules,— do of right belong and appertain, as appears from the Records of my Office, unto the **Provost, Fellows and Scholars of the College of the Holy and Undivided Trinity of Queen Elizabeth near Dublin** and their successors for ever, according to the Laws of Arms.

As Witness my hand and Seal this tenth day of January in the Sixty fourth year of the Reign of Our Sovereign Lady Victoria by the Grace of God of the United Kingdom of Great Britain and Ireland, Queen, Defender of the Faith, and so forth and in the year of Our Lord One thousand nine hundred and one.

Arthur E Vicars Ulster King of Arms of All Ireland

Trinity
"This place that's always fresh and new"

Although Trinity College is more than four hundred years old, its most striking characteristic is its elegant and vibrant youthfulness. I've often wondered what are the reasons for its youthfulness.

The first reason is the constant, ever-changing tide of people moving through the College. I don't just mean the students, but also the teaching, security and administrative staff, the convivial workers who keep the college spick and span, and the endless visitors looking about them with wonder on their faces as they consider the old buildings or scrutinise the Book of Kells. This old-young College has a mesmeric character and is a source of unfailing interest. "I could never get enough of Trinity" a woman who graduated some twenty years ago said to me recently when she made a return visit to College. "There's something about this place that's always fresh and new."

Fresh and new. Every October, thousands of excited, adventurous and slightly nervous undergraduates come to Trinity and replace the thousands who have just graduated. These annual injections of adventurous excitement can be savoured during Freshers' Week in Front Square, when amid slogans, shouts, banners, competitive frenzy and unbridled exhortations, these new students choose the Societies which they wish to join in College. Freshers' Week is a delightfully boisterous beginning to any undergraduate's career. Everyone enjoys it.

Paradoxically, even the most ancient of the College buildings contributes to Trinity's youthfulness. These buildings are scrupulously preserved, constantly used, and have a stylish, dignified and enduring character all their own. The centuries weigh lightly on them. They are full of history but not burdened by it. They are strikingly handsome but not heavily solemn. They even seem, in their own gracious, patient way, to encourage that sense of youthful intellectual adventure. They are guardians of vitality and protectors of dreams.

I love the mix of fields and buildings in Trinity; a perfect example, at the beginning of the twenty-first century, of *rus in urbe*. Though the College is surrounded by a wall, this mixture of fields and buildings, of grass and stone, of sports and study creates a climate of relaxed freedom in the middle of a busy city which is a joy to experience at any hour of the day or night.

Trinity has a genuinely friendly atmosphere. It is always possible to have an enjoyable conversation, hear stimulating stories and be part of a vital community in which public togetherness is relished and necessary solitude respected. Learning is a lifelong adventure; this fact is recognised and encouraged in Trinity. This recognition and encouragement continues to deepen and expand. The place never stops growing. That's the most dynamic sign of an ancient place with a youthful spirit. It is an inspiring example to us all.

Though a Senior Fellow and Professor of Modern Literature, **Brendan Kennelly** is a poet and Kerryman upon whom "the centuries weigh lightly".

previous pages:
2. 'Domini Doctores' in procession
page 6:
3. Trinity College Crest.

4

5

previous pages:
4. The West Front, completed 1759
these pages:
5. The Campanile (19th cent.) from Front Gate
6. Keeping warm
7. Front Gate, with Oliver Goldsmith

6

7

8. Freshers' Week in Front Square
9. Join the Juggling Society!
10. Front Square in Freshers' Week
11. Front Gate

12

13

14

12. Strawberries and cream in the Provost's Garden
14 & 16. Madrigals and minuets at the College Garden Party

13. The Provost's House (18th cent.) from the Garden
15. The Provost's House - Number One, Grafton Street

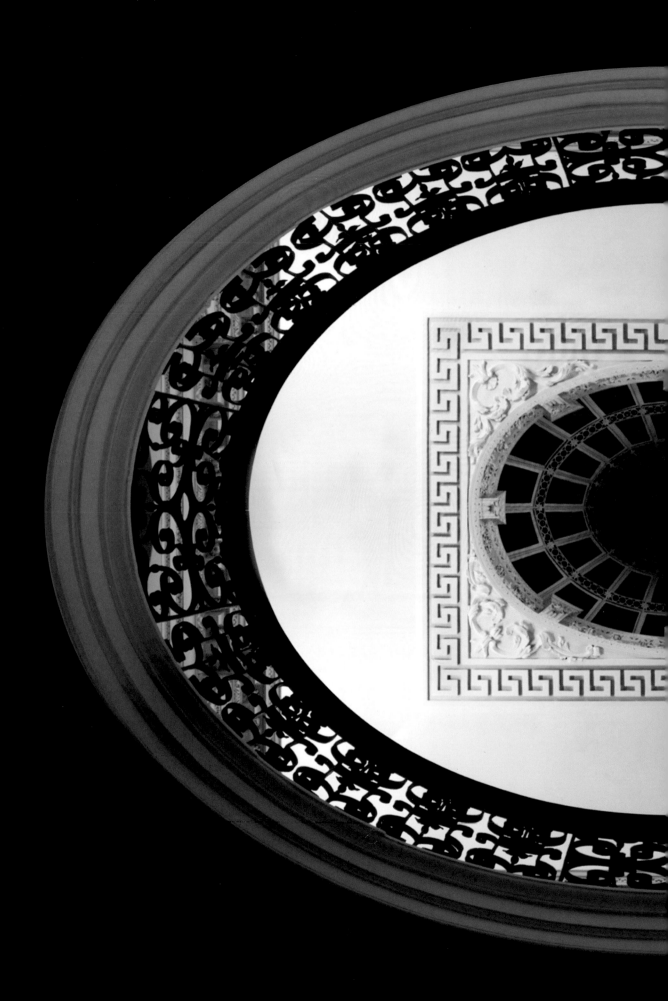

19

20

22

23

previous pages:
17. The Provost's House, top landing
these pages:
18. The Saloon of the Provost's House
19. The Dining Room of the Provost's House
20—23. Details of 18th century plasterwork in the Provost's House

24

SEEK YE FIRST THE KINGDOM OF GOD AND HIS RIGHTEOUSNESS

WHEN · THE · MULTITUDE · HEARD · THEY
WERE · ASTONISHED · AT · HIS · DOCTRINE

✠ IN · MEM · OF · THE · Rᵗ · REVᵈ · GEORGE · BERKELEY · Dᵈᴰ · BISHOP
OF · LOYNE · SOMETIME · FELLOW · OF · THIS · 1710

25

previous pages:
24. The College Chapel in Front Square, designed by Chambers in the 18th century
these pages:
25. Berkeley memorial stained glass window in College Chapel
26. Interior of the 18th century College Chapel

26

27

28

29

30

32. The Gallery Chapel, opened in 1976
33. The narthex, or porch, of the College Chapel

33

34. Magnolia in bloom, Trinity Term

35. Interior of the Public Theatre (the Exam Hall). Designed by Chambers in the 18th century
36. Front Square on Trinity Monday
37. The 18th century Baldwin Monument in the Public Theatre
38. The Hall of Honour and 1937 Reading Room in Front Square

39

39—42. Trinity Ball

40

41

43

43. Front Square
45. An evening view of the Arts Building

44. The Campanile and Graduates' Memorial Building
46. The Buttery

47. The 18th century Dining Hall
49. The Common Room
48 & 50. The Atrium, designed by de Blacam & Meagher (1986)

48

49

50

52

previous pages:
51. Interior of the 18th century Dining Hall (restored after a serious fire in 1984)
The College Mace is placed on High Table
these pages:
52. View from the 19th century Campanile towards Front Gate
53. View from the Campanile towards the Rubrics (c.1700)
54—56. Carved heads on the keystones of the Campanile arches
(54. Demosthenes, 55. Socrates, 56. Homer. Plato is not shown)

53

54

55

56

57. The Old Library, designed by Burgh in the early 18th century, seen from Fellows' Square (formerly the Fellows' Garden)

58

59

60

61

58—61. Details from the Old Library:
58. Ironwork spiral staircase
59. 18th century bust of William Shakespeare
60. The Brian Boru Harp
61. Carved detail of staircase (1720s)
62. The barrel-vaulted Long Room of the Old Library. (18th and 19th cent.)

63. & 64. Pages from the Book of Kells, a 9th century illuminated manuscript of the Four Gospels

65. The 18th century Old Library reflected in the Arts and Social Sciences Building, which was designed by Paul Koralek and opened in 1978

66. The Arts Building from Fellows' Square 67. Calder's *Cactus* (1967) in Fellows' Square
68. Arts Building roof garden 69. The Edmund Burke Theatre in the Arts Building

70

71

72

70—72. International art at the Douglas Hyde Gallery:
70. Dhruva Mistry   71. Tony Oursler & Sadie Benning
72. David Nash   73. The Arts Building from College Park

74. Oregon Maple; the Old Library in the background
75. A mistle thrush nests in a College tree
76. Library Square in Trinity Term; Rubrics in the background
77. Time out in Fellows' Square; Arts Building in background

74

75

76

77

78. Botany Bay. Designed by Morrison, completed in 1817
79. Living in Rooms, Botany Bay
80. Ginger, the College Cat
81. Daffodils in Hilary Term
82. Library Square

83. The Graduates' Memorial Building (GMB)
Designed by Drew and completed in 1902
84—86. GMB details

84

85

86

87. The New Library, as it will appear from College Park
88. Aerial view of the New Library. Designed by Keane Murphy Duff/McCullough Mulvin and due to open in 2001

89 & 90. Two views in Fellows' Square; Koralek's Berkeley Library (1967) on the left and his Arts Building (1978)

91. New Square, showing the entrance to Number 39 (1840)

92. The Printing House in New Square, designed by Castle in the 1730s

93—95. Near the Museum Building:
93. Pomodoro's *Sphere with Sphere* (1982-83) on the podium of the Berkeley Library in New Square
94. Thornton's 20th century marble, *Untitled*, at the corner of College Park
95. Between the Rubrics and the Old Library, steps are seen leading to the podium of the Berkeley Library

96–99. The Rubrics, Trinity's oldest surviving building, was begun around 1700.
At the east end of Library Square, it looks out on to New Square
97. Dutch gable on the Rubrics
98. Stone lintel to Number 26

99

100

100. The Museum Building (Deane, Woodward & Deane, 1854-57) viewed from College Park

102

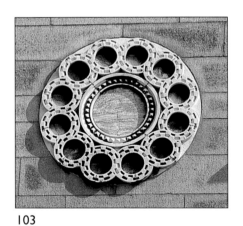

103

104

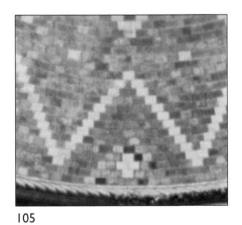

105

101—105. The Museum Building - details:

102. Arches above the balconies

104. Carved stone decoration

101. The Main Hall

103. Venetian-style exterior wall plaques

105. Domed ceiling of enameled brick

106

106. The Museum Building doorway at dusk
107 & 108. Museum Building
seen from College Park
109. The Giant Irish Deer skeleton in the
Museum Building

111

112

113

114

115. College Park- the Rugby Pitch with, from left,
House No. 38; the Beckett Theatre;
House Nos.47—52 (residences, Day Nursery and Student Health Centre)
and Drew's Engineering Laboratory.

116. The Civil Engineering Building
117. The serpentine at
Aras an Phiarsigh
118. The Map Library
119. The Beckett Theatre and
Centre for the Performing
Arts (de Blacam & Meagher
1991)

120

121

122

120. Runner in College Park   121 & 122. The Moyne Institute   123. Rugby in College Park

125

124. Snow in College Park
125. The Pavilion in the snow
126. Testing...
127. Parsons Podium

126

127

128

128. The Physics Building , designed by Marshall in 1904
130. The Anatomy Theatre

129. The Dixon Laboratory entrance
131. Early anatomists

129

130

131

132. The Sami Nas'r Institute of Advanced Materials Science; Chemistry Building on the right

133. Prof. E.T.S. Walton's Nobel Medal
     for Physics (1951)
134 & 135. Science laboratories

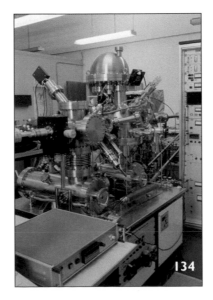

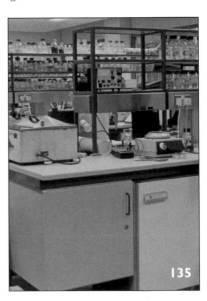

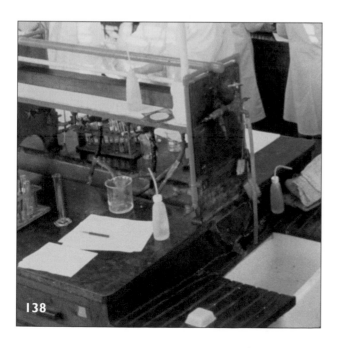

136—138. Science laboratories
139 The Botany Building, designed by Marshall in 1906

139

140

141

142

In the Zoology Museum: 140—142. Blaschka's 19th century glass specimens:
140. Sea anemone *Hormathia digitata*   141. Protozoan
142. Sea anemone *Scolianthus callimorphus*   and 143. White-tailed eagle

144. Banana tree in the O'Reilly Institute
145. The Arches, near Pearse Station
146. The O'Reilly Institute, from Westland Row
147 & 148. The Hamilton Building
149. Glass bridge to the Biochemistry Building
150. The Atrium of the O'Reilly Institute

151—153. The Smurfit Institute of
Genetics
152. Pomodoro's *Dreams* in the
Genetics Institute
154. Entrance to the Panoz Institute and
School of Pharmacy

155

156

157

155. The Dental Hospital and School of Dental
    Science in Lincoln Place
156. Light sculpture by Lindsey Bloxham in the Dental
    Hospital
157. Dental science students at work
158. Koralek's 1998 Dental Hospital is linked to the
    Victorian façade

158

159. Westland Row
160. The Clocktower at 8 Westland Square
161. Goldsmith Hall and its glass bridge over Westland Row
162. Foster Place   163. Trinity Enterprise Centre in Pearse Street

164

165

164. The School of Nursing and Midwifery Studies and the Haughton Institute at St James's

165. Entrance to the Trinity College Centre for Health Sciences at St James's Hospital

166. Pomodoro's bronze plaque for the entrance to St James's Hospital, Phase II

166

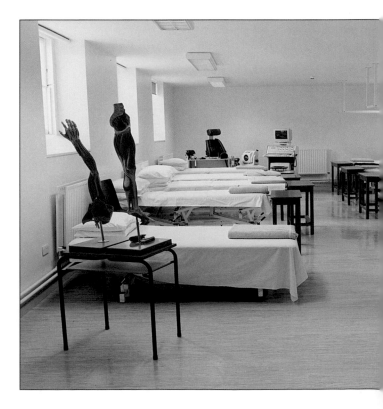

167. Teaching ward at the School of Physiotherapy, Trinity College Centre for Health Sciences, St James's

168 & 169. The Trinity College Centre for Health Sciences in the Adelaide and Meath Hospitals incorporating the National Children's Hospital at Tallaght

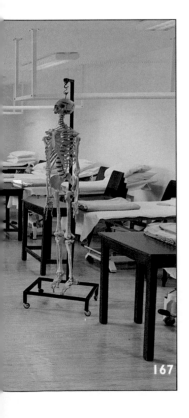

170

170 & 172. The College Botanic Gardens
        at Trinity Hall, Dartry
171. Botanical drawing of an orchid,
        dated 1894
173. Head of the River
174. The River Liffey and the Boathouse
        at Islandbridge

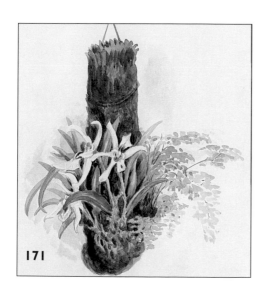

171

172

175 & 176 Fireworks in Front Square celebrating the College's Quatercentenary in Trinity Week 1992

Heading out to Front Square

Trinity College Dublin

— A Beautiful Place

About the Illustrations

1. Henry Moore's *Reclining Connected Forms* (1969) in the January light. The view is southwestwards across Library Square, between the western end of the Old Library and the Campanile, towards the 1937 Reading Room.

2. 'Domini Doctores' in procession. Front Square, with the Chapel, the Graduates' Memorial Building and the Campanile. Candidates for doctoral degrees process towards Commencements ceremony, conducted entirely in Latin, in the Examination Hall.

3. Trinity College Crest. The armorial bearings granted to 'the Provost, Fellows and Scholars of the College of the Holy and Undivided Trinity… near Dublin.'

4. The West Front of Trinity looks on to College Green. It was constructed between 1752 and 1759, to a design attributed to Theodore Jacobsen.

5. The Campanile (19th century) from Front Gate. This elegant bell-tower, which houses the College bell, was designed by Charles Lanyon in the 1850s.

6. Keeping warm. A pigeon keeps warm on one of the lights inside the arch at Front Gate.

7. Front Gate, with Oliver Goldsmith. The Front Gate on the College Green side is flanked by statues of two of TCD's distinguished 18th century alumni: poet and playwright Oliver Goldsmith (1728-74) and Edmund Burke (1729-97), orator and political philosopher. The life-size statues, by John Henry Foley, were erected by public subscription in the 1860s.

8. Freshers' Week in Front Square. Every year in October, the week before lectures begin in Michaelmas Term is marked by this 'delightfully boisterous beginning to any undergraduate's career', as student societies vie with each other to attract new members.

9. Join the Juggling Society! More than 80 student societies cover a vast spectrum of interests.

10. Front Square in Freshers' Week. Among the flourishing societies are the 'Phil', the University Philosophical Society (founded 1684), the 'Hist', the College Historical Society (founded 1770) and 'Choral', the University of Dublin Choral Society (founded 1837).

11. Front Gate. This is the familiar pedestrian entrance on College Green.

12. Strawberries and cream in the Provost's Garden. A highlight of the Trinity Week celebrations in May each year is the elegant Garden Party.

13. The Provost's House (18th century) from the Garden. One of the most splendid and perfectly preserved of Dublin's 18th century residences, the Provost's House cost £11,000 to build in the 1760s.

14 & 16. Madrigals and minuets at the College Garden Party. Members of College Chapel Choir entertain guests in a sylvan setting.

15. The Provost's House—Number One, Grafton Street. Apart from the addition of the Provost's Library in the 1770s, there has been no major alteration to the House over the years.

17. The Provost's House, top landing. Daylight falls from this pretty oval lantern on to a gallery surrounded by Turner's wrought iron balustrade.

18. The Saloon of the Provost's House. The main reception room in the Provost's House, this lovely Palladian room occupies the whole of the first floor at the front.

19. The Dining Room of the Provost's House. The outstanding plasterwork throughout the House is by Patrick and John Wall.

20—23. Details of 18th century plasterwork in the Provost's House

24. The College Chapel in Front Square. In 1775, William Chambers designed this graceful classical ensemble of buildings, where the matching Corinthian temple fronts of the College Chapel and the Examination Hall address each other across the cobbles of Front Square.

25. Berkeley memorial stained glass window in College Chapel. This window is in memory of Bishop George Berkeley (1685-1753), one of the most influential classical philosophers, who was a student and teacher at Trinity. It depicts the Sermon on the Mount, and Christ in discussion with the teachers of the Law.

26. Interior of the 18th century College Chapel. The design of the Chapel mirrors that of the Examination Hall (see no. 35).

27—31. Details of the 18th century College Chapel:
27. The lantern over the entrance;
28. The fine plasterwork is by the famous 18th century stuccodore, Michael Stapleton;
29. The rear pews, formerly reserved for Senior Fellows and resident Masters, have carved wooden arm rests;
30. The interior with its original collegiate pews has changed little since 1798. The tiled

floor and heating grilles are 19th century additions;
31. The organ originally designed by Green, George III's favourite organ builder, was almost completely rebuilt by Telford in 1842. In 1968, a new organ, designed by Ralph Downes was built by Walker of London. With its splendid 18th century Caribbean mahogany case, it offers a stunning counterpoint to the stained glass windows at the east end of the chapel.

32. The Gallery Chapel, opened in 1976. Since 1973, the Chapel has been used by all religious denominations.

33. The narthex of the College Chapel, through which worshippers have entered daily throughout term for over 200 years.

34. Magnolia in bloom, Trinity Term. A view

of East Chapel through the *Magnolia x soulangiana* in blossom.

35. Interior of the Public Theatre (the Examination Hall). Matching the Chapel interior (see no. 26), the plasterwork is by Michael Stapleton. Built between 1777 and the mid-1780s, to a design by William Chambers.

36. Front Square on Trinity Monday. From the steps of the Exam Hall, at 10 a.m. on Trinity Monday each year in May, the Provost, surrounded by the Board in formal academic gowns and hoods, announces the names of new Fellows and Scholars, who then become members of the body corporate of the College.

37. The 18th century Baldwin Monument in the Public Theatre. This Carrara marble monument by Hewetson can be seen inside the Exam Hall, against the right-hand wall. Restored in 1991, it is in memory of Richard Baldwin, Provost for 41 years from 1717.

38. The Hall of Honour and 1937 Reading Room in Front Square. An octagonal galleried reading room is behind the Hall of Honour. Designed by Sir Thomas Drew in 1920, it commemorates members of College who died in war; among them is the architect's son, who died at Gallipoli.

39—42. Trinity Ball. The Trinity Week Ball has been held on the College campus since 1959. It concludes an annual week of sporting and social events, beginning with Trinity Monday (see no. 36), which celebrates the historic foundation of the College.

43. Front Square. The view from the Dining Hall steps towards the 1937 Reading Room.

44. The Campanile and Graduates' Memorial Building (the GMB). The GMB, designed by Sir Thomas Drew, opened in 1902 on the site of the former Rotten Row. It incorporates residential wings and major societies' rooms.

45. Coming from the Arts Building. An evening view of the Arts and Social Sciences Building, with the Old Library on the left and the 1937 Reading Room on the right.

46. The Buttery. Opened in 1963, in the old cellars of the Dining Hall, the Buttery is a popular gathering place.

47. The 18th century Dining Hall.

The Dining Hall, originally designed by Richard Castle, was rebuilt c. 1760 by Hugh Darley.

48 & 50. The Atrium, This modern atrium adjoining the Dining Hall was created by the Dublin architects de Blacam & Meagher in 1986, within the shell of the 18th century kitchen.

49. The Common Room. Of Palladian design, situated on the first floor of the Dining Hall, the staff Common Room faces south into Front Square.

51. Interior of the 18th century Dining Hall (restored after a serious fire in 1984). The College Mace is placed on High Table. The Dining Hall, here set for a formal dinner, is in daily use throughout term, as students and staff dine together each evening on Commons. Grace in Latin, in a form prescribed by Provost Bedell in 1627, is repeated before and after meat by a Scholar of the House. The silver College Mace, displayed, as here, or carried in procession on ceremonial occasions, was made in Dublin c. 1708 by Thomas Bolton.

52. View from the 19th century Campanile towards Front Square.

53. View from the Campanile towards the Rubrics (c.1700) . The Campanile, erected in 1855, was designed by Lanyon. Its Great Bell, cast in 1742, hung formerly in a domed bell-tower designed by Castle but removed, for safety reasons in 1791. The smaller, or 'Provost's Bell', cast in the 14th or 15th century, probably came from the steeple of All Hallows Priory, the monastery site upon which the College was established in 1592.

54—56. Carved heads on the keystones of the Campanile arches, recently identified by JV Luce: 54 Demosthenes, 55 Socrates, 56 Homer. (Plato is not shown).

57. The Old Library, seen from Fellows' Square (formerly the Fellows' Garden). Designed by Thomas Burgh and built

between 1712 and 1732, it houses the Book of Kells, early printed books and manuscripts and a modern conservation laboratory.

58—61. Details from the Old Library:
58. Ironwork spiral staircase;
59. 18th century bust of William Shakespeare - one of 14 attributed to Peter Scheemakers, part of Dr Gilbert's bequest in the 1840s;
60. The Brian Boru Harp. The oldest known example of the medieval Irish Harp, it is made of willow, with metal strings which were plucked with long fingernails;
61. Carved detail of one of the finest two small staircases in Ireland (1720s).

62. The Long Room of the Old Library. This spectacular architecture was created when, in 1860, Deane & Woodward added the gallery bookcases and the barrel vault to Burgh's early 18th century gallery front and lower bookcases.

63 & 64. Pages from the Book of Kells, a 9th century illuminated manuscript of the Four Gospels:
63. A concordance or canon table;
64. Portrait of Christ (fol.32v).

65—69. The Arts Building; Fellows' Square; Calder's *Cactus* (1967); Arts Building roof garden; the Burke Theatre. Designed by Paul Koralek and opened in 1978, the Arts and Social Sciences Building incorporates a number of roof gardens. It bounds Fellows' Square, the former Fellows' Garden, where the steel stabile, *Cactus*, (1967) by Alexander Calder is displayed. Its five major lecture theatres are named after famous graduates: Edmund Burke(1748);James Ussher (1598); Jonathan Swift (1686); Thomas Davis (1836) and Ernest Walton (1926). A large chamber (of computers for student use) is named after Samuel Beckett (1927) and a library after WEH Lecky (1859).

70—72. The Douglas Hyde Gallery. This modern art gallery at the Nassau Street entrance to the Arts Building is named after Douglas Hyde (1862-1949), Irish scholar and first President of Ireland, a Trinity graduate of 1884. Opened in 1978, the DHG has become one of the chief venues in Ireland for temporary exhibitions of Irish and international modern art.

73. The Arts Building from College Park.

74. Oregon Maple. One of two, possibly the oldest trees in College,

In Front Square after Commencements

Provost Salmon

planted before 1850, the *Acer macrophyllum*, with the Old Library in the background.

75. A mistle thrush nests in a College tree. Many birds make their home in Trinity's urban arboretum.

76. Library Square in Trinity Term; Rubrics in the background.

77. Time out in Fellows' Square; Arts Building in background. The former Fellows' Garden, with its vista of the Provost's House, is bounded on the south side by the Arts Building (1978). Trinity Term croquet matches formerly played here now take place in New Square.

78. Botany Bay. A residential square behind the GMB, designed by Richard Morrison and completed in 1817, it is probably so named after the old kitchen gardens. Hard tennis courts were laid in 1955.

79. Living in Rooms, Botany Bay. Trinity has always been a residential college; rooms were modernised and furnished in the 1960s.

80. Ginger, the College Cat. Ginger, a marmalade tom, mysteriously disappeared from his College habitat in early 2000.

81. Daffodils in Hilary Term. Since 1834, the Trinity academic year has been divided into three terms: Hilary Term (January-April) takes its name from St Hilary's Day, 13 January, and Trinity Term (April-July) from the Feast of the Holy Trinity, eight weeks after Easter. The academic year opens in September in Michaelmas Term, named after the Feast of St Michael and All Angels, 29 September.

82. Library Square. The red-berried *Cotoneaster salicifolius*, with the Old Library in the background.

83. The Graduates' Memorial Building (GMB). Designed by Sir Thomas Drew and completed in 1902, the GMB adds a touch of late Victorian style to the ensemble of Front and Library Squares.

84—86. GMB details. Flanked by residential wings Numbers 28 and 30, the GMB, behind its handsome door (85), houses the major student debating societies, the 'Hist' and the 'Phil'.

87 & 88. Two views of the new Library. Designed in 1999 by Keane Murphy Duff/McCullough Mulvin, the new £16m Library and Research Information Centre, due to open in 2001, will join the existing Lecky and Berkeley Libraries.

89 & 90. Two views in Fellows' Square. Paul Koralek's landmark Berkeley Library (1967) and his Arts and Social Sciences Building (1978), which incorporated a new entrance to the College from Nassau Street.

91. New Square, showing the entrance to Number 39 (1840). Law lectures are given in Number 39, home of the School of Mathematics from 1930-92. Samuel Beckett lived here as an undergraduate, and referred to it in his first novel, *A Dream of Fair to Middling Women*.

92. The Printing House in New Square, designed by Richard Castle in 1734, in the style of a Greek temple.

93—95. Near the Museum Building:
Surrounded by beautiful 18th, 19th and 20th century buildings, the elevated podium of the Berkeley Library stands at the junction of College Park, New Square and Fellows' Square. Pomodoro's *Sphere with sphere* (1982-83) is a familiar landmark;
94. Thornton's 20th century marble, *Untitled*, at the corner of College Park;
95. Between the Rubrics and the Old Library, steps are seen leading to the podium of the Berkeley Library.

Clock on the Dining Hall Façade

Window of GMB

Challoner's Corner behind the Chapel, six Provosts are buried here

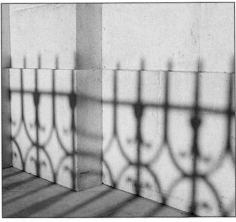

Shadows in the Chapel Porch

Fireplace in the Provost's House

Anthropoid clay coffin lid from Lachish,
circa 1200 BC, at the Weingreen Museum

96—99. The Rubrics, Trinity's oldest surviving building, was begun around 1700. At the east end of Library Square, it also looks out on to New Square, and continues as student and staff residences:

97 The striking Dutch gables were created when the top floor was rebuilt in the 1890s;

98 Stone lintel to Number 26. Oliver Goldsmith lived in the Rubrics as an undergraduate, in a part of Number 22, now demolished, which adjoined the Old Library (see picture no.95).

100. The Museum Building viewed from College Park. Designed by Deane & Woodward (1854-57) in Gothic Revival style, this is one of Ireland's finest 19th century buildings. It houses departments of civil engineering, geology and geography.

101—105. The Museum Building—details:

101. The Main Hall displays columns of eleven different Irish marbles. On their Portland stone capitals can be seen, carved by the O'Shea Brothers of Cork in the 19th century, plants and wild creatures from the College Botanic Garden, then in Ballsbridge;

102 & 105. In the graceful curves and colours of the interior can be detected Moorish elements, recalling the Great Mosque at Cordova.

103, 104, 107, 108. The building takes its Venetian style from elements such as the grouping of its windows (see 107 &108), its carved detail (104) and these exterior marble discs (103) from two *palazzi* in Venice.

106. The Museum Building doorway at dusk. The oak door is surmounted by the College crest.

107 & 108. Museum Building seen from College Park.

109. The Giant Irish Deer skeleton in the Museum Building. The entrance hall is dominated by a pair of skeletons of the Giant Irish Deer or 'Great Elk'.

110. New Square in Michaelmas Term. Autumn leaves cover the grass of the garden retreat beside Number 40 created by the American garden designer Lanning Roper (1912-83). Nassau Street buildings are seen in the distance.

111. Soccer Match in College Park. The Dublin University Association Football Club was founded in 1884; Trinity colours are red and black.

112. 'Chariots of Fire'. Inspired by the film 'Chariots of Fire', a race run against the Campanile bell has become a Trinity Week tradition.

113. Black Belts. The Luce Hall, designed by Scott Tallon Walker and opened in 1981-82, accommodates gymnasium and indoor sports. Extensive sports facilities also exist at Santry, near Dublin Airport, including synthetic grass surfaces.

114. Cricket in College Park. The Trinity Cricket Club was founded in 1835, but the cricket pitch was not laid out until 1842.

115. This view of College Park shows the Rugby Pitch with, from left: Number 38, beside the Narrows gateway; the Beckett Theatre; Numbers 47-52. built in 1991/92 to incorporate student residences, the Student Health Centre (established 1964) and the College Day Nursery (established 1970). Drew's 19th century Engineering Laboratory is on the right.

116. The Civil Engineering Building, an extension to Drew's Engineering Laboratory, almost one hundred years later.

117. The serpentine entrance area to Áras an Phiarsigh, beside the Beckett Theatre on the left. In 1996, the architects Moloney O'Beirne and Partners won an RIAI award for transforming a modern office block on the site of

Plasterwork in Regent House

the old Queen's Theatre on Pearse Street and re-aligning it with the geometry of the street.

118. The Map Library. The College Map Library holds the largest collection of printed maps in Ireland.

119. The Samuel Beckett Theatre and Centre for the Performing Arts, and adjoining houses (see 115 above), were designed by Dublin architects de Blacam & Meagher as part of the Pearse Street Development in 1991.

120. Runner in College Park. Various types of athletics, football, hurling, and other traditional Irish sports, have been played in College Park since the 18th century.

121 & 122. The Moyne Institute. Designed by Desmond Fitzgerald, the Moyne Institute was opened in 1953 by the donor, the Marchioness of Normanby, in memory of her father, Lord Moyne. A Y-shaped building on the corner of College Park, it houses the microbiology department. It was extended in 1981, and substantially expanded with the creation of new laboratories, below ground level, in the mid-1990s.

123. Rugby in College Park. The rugby pitch was laid out in 1901, but the oldest continuously existing rugby club in the world is probably in Trinity: the Football Club formed in 1854. More than 150 Trinity rugby players have represented Ireland. The College First XV wear white jerseys.

124. Snow in College Park. Late snowfall on the blossom of the double wild cherry tree in College Park.

125. The Pavilion in the snow. The Pavilion in College Park was designed by Sir

Thomas Drew and opened in 1885. A wing was added in 1920 and another in 1961.

126. Testing… A mechanical engineering student at work in the Parsons Building (formerly the Pathology Department.)

127. Parsons Podium. This extension, just inside Lincoln Place Gate, won architectural awards in 1996. The department of Mechanical and Manufacturing Engineering is located in the Parsons Building, which was designed in 1895.

128. The Physics Building, designed by WC Marshall in 1904, with a major extension in the 1960s. A blue plaque commemorates Professor Ernest Walton, Nobel Prize-winning nuclear physicist.

129. The Dixon Laboratory. Designed by FG Hicks and opened in 1939, the former Dixon Hall commemorated a distinguished professor of botany, Henry Dixon. The

Scrolls supporting Regent House landing, by P. & J. Wall

laboratory and the Portland stone sculpture panels (1938/39) by Wilfred Dudeney, representing Wonder and Aspiration, are incorporated into the Institute of Advanced Materials Science (Sami Nas'r).

130. The Anatomy Theatre. An 'Elaboratory' for anatomy was first opened in Trinity in 1711, and lectureships were established at the time in anatomy, chemistry and botany.

131. Early anatomists; painted panel in the Anatomy Department. Practical considerations in earlier years would explain the banishment of Anatomy to the edge of the built-up area of College.

132—138. The Institute of Advanced Materials Science (Sami Nas'r): Chemistry Building on the right. Adjoining the Physics (1904) and Botany (1906) buildings, the new Institute of Advanced Materials Science (2000) forms a major part of the developing Physical Sciences Complex at the East End of College.

133. Prof. ETS Walton's Nobel Medal. Ernest Walton (1903-95), student and professor in Trinity, was awarded the Nobel Prize for Physics in 1951 for 'splitting the atom', with John Cockcroft at the Cavendish Laboratory in Cambridge in 1932.

139. The Botany Building, designed in 1906 by WC Marshall, architect of the Physics Building (1906).

140—142. In the Zoology Museum: Bohemian glassworkers and naturalists, Leopold Blaschka and his son Rudolf, using secret techniques, made, in Dresden, thousands of these exquisite marine models between 1863 and 1890. Their magnificent glass flower specimens are on display at the botanical museum in Harvard University.

Walking under the Campanile

Blaschka's 19th century glass specimens:
140. Sea anemone *Hormathia digitata*;
141. Protozoan;
142. Sea anemone *Scolianthus callimorphus*.

143. White-tailed eagle A specimen donated recently to the Zoology Museum, this native sea-eagle, now extinct, was shot in Cork in the late 1800s.

144 & 150. Banana tree in the O'Reilly Institute. The fructiferous tree is one of a number of tropical specimens in the atrium garden of the O'Reilly Institute for Communications and Technology, facing on to Westland Row opposite Pearse Station.

145. The Arches, near Pearse Station. Under the railway lines are banks of computers for students' use.

146. The O'Reilly Institute, from Westland Row. This was designed by Scott Tallon Walker and opened in 1989.

147 & 148. The Hamilton Building. This building, behind Westland Row, was opened in 1992 and commemorates William Rowan Hamilton, one of the world's greatest mathematicians, who graduated from Trinity in 1827.

149. Glass bridge to the Biochemistry Building, linking it to the Hamilton Building.

150. The Atrium of the O'Reilly Institute.

151—153. The Smurfit Institute of Genetics, beside Lincoln Place Gate, was opened in 1998. It is linked via a glass atrium to the houses in Westland Row which are used as offices and seminar rooms.

152. Arnaldo Pomodoro's eight panels, *Dreams*, embellish the Genetics Institute.

154. Entrance to the Panoz Institute and School of Pharmacy. The School of Pharmacy was established in Trinity in 1977, and has been in these new premises since 1998.

155—158. The Dental Hospital in Lincoln Place, founded in 1895, contains the School of Dental Science, and sees 2,500 patients a week. In 1999, Ahrends, Burton & Koralek won a European award for their design, which incorporates the Victorian building.
156. Light sculpture by Lindsey Bloxham in the Dental Hospital.
157. Dental science students at work.
158. Koralek's 1998 Dental Hospital is linked to the Victorian facade.

159. Westland Row. Number 21 Westland Row, the birthplace of Oscar Wilde, a former Trinity student, houses the University's Oscar Wilde Centre for Irish Writing.

160 & 161. The Clocktower at 8 Westland Square. At the eastern end of the College campus areas suitable for development and expansion have been acquired: No. 8 Westland Square, and the former An Post site adjoining Goldsmith Hall and Pearse Station.

161. Goldsmith Hall (late 1990s), incorporating student residences, society rooms and lecture halls, is linked by the glass bridge to the main campus.

162. Foster Place. To facilitate expansion of its city centre location, Trinity has acquired all the six fine Georgian houses in Foster Place in College Green.

163. Trinity Enterprise Centre in Pearse Street. Trinity purchased, for increased research and development space, the Enterprise Centre in Pearse Street, from the Industrial Development Authority. Seven minutes' walk from the existing Innovation Centre in the O'Reilly Institute, it contains this protected building, the Tower, which is a craft centre.

164—169. Established in 1994, the Trinity College Centre for Health Sciences operates at St James's Hospital, Dublin, and at the Adelaide and Meath Hospitals, incorporating the National Children's Hospital, at Tallaght. The faculty encompasses nine health professions: Clinical Speech and Language, Dentistry, Dietetics, Medicine, Midwifery, Nursing, Physiotherapy, Occupational Therapy and Therapeutic Radiography. The Haughton Institute for postgraduate educational research in Health Sciences is jointly owned by Trinity, St James's Hospital and the new teaching hospital at Tallaght.

164. The School of Nursing and Midwifery Studies and the Haughton Institute at St James's.

165. Entrance to the Trinity College Centre for Health Sciences at St James's Hospital.

166. Pomodoro's bronze plaque for the entrance to St James's Hospital, Phase II.

167. Teaching ward at the School of Physiotherapy, Trinity College Centre for Health Sciences, St James's.

168 & 169. The Trinity College Centre for Health Sciences in the Adelaide and Meath Hospitals incorporating the National Children's Hospital at Tallaght.

170 & 172. The College Botanic Gardens at Trinity Hall, Dartry. Trinity has an unbroken tradition of cultivated gardens since its foundation in 1592. The Botanic Garden was situated in Ballsbridge from 1806 until 1968, when it was removed to the present site. Trinity Hall, a residential Hall purchased in 1908, and originally exclusively for women students, has been much expanded. Women were admitted to Trinity in 1904.

171. This botanical drawing of an orchid, *Leptotes bicolor / / lindl.*, dated '21.i.1894' is in the School of Botany, TCD.

173. Head of the River. Dublin University Boat Club was formed in 1867 and in 1898, at a suitable stretch of the River Liffey at Islandbridge, the river-bank was straightened and this boathouse erected. The College Regatta takes place here in Trinity Term. DU Boat Club colours are black and white with the College crest in blue.

174. The River Liffey and the Boathouse (at Islandbridge).

175 & 176. Fireworks in Front Square celebrating the College's Quatercentenary in Trinity Week 1992. Trinity College celebrated its first 400 years in 1992. The opening of Quatercentenary week on 9 May 1992 was heralded with a spectacular firework display in Front Square.

Doors on Pearse Street

The Campanile Cross